A MESSAGE TO FAMILIES AND FRIENDS

I0502805

Cancer free is a coloring book to honor families and friends who went through the struggles in fighting cancer. It's time to appreciate them and honor their fight against cancer because they are cancer free.Being alive with your loved ones is the greatest gift and blessing of all! Let's Fight Cancer!

FROM YOUR AUTHOR
BTARTIST

Cancer

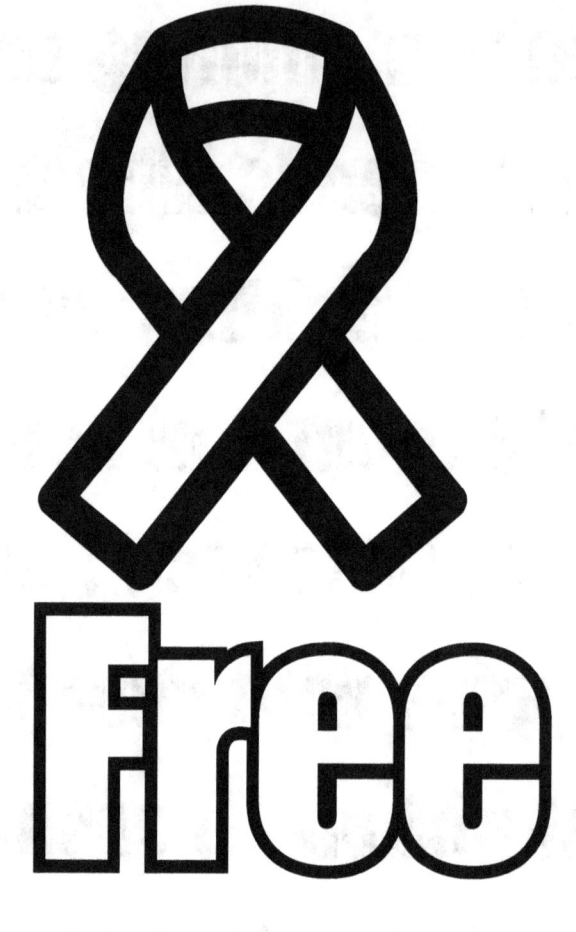

Free

Your Author
BTArtist

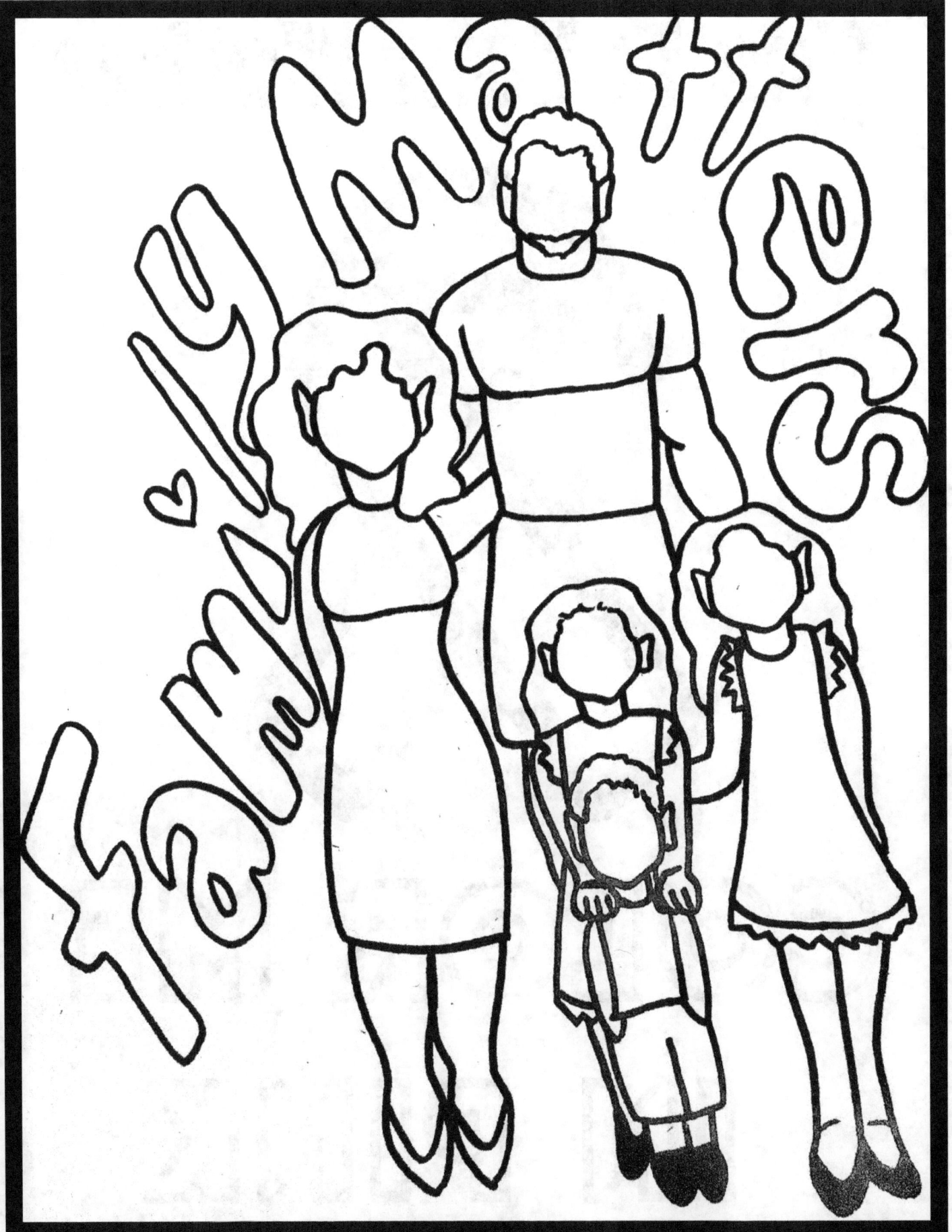

This Is Your Mother

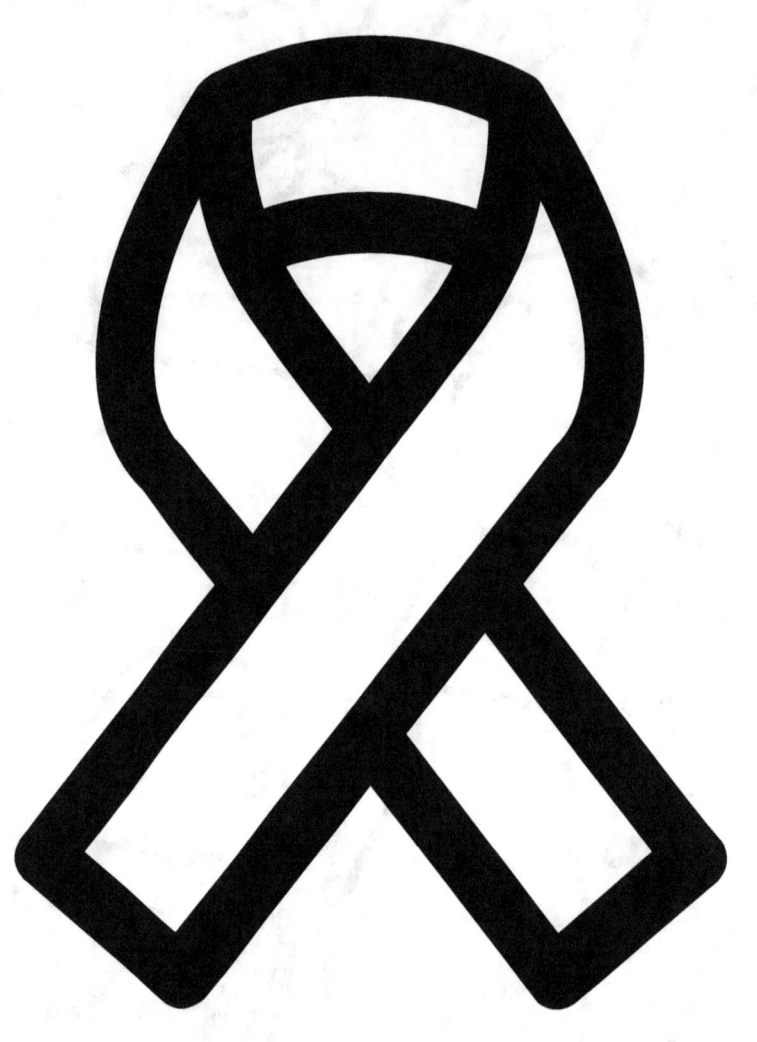

COLOR ME IN PINK

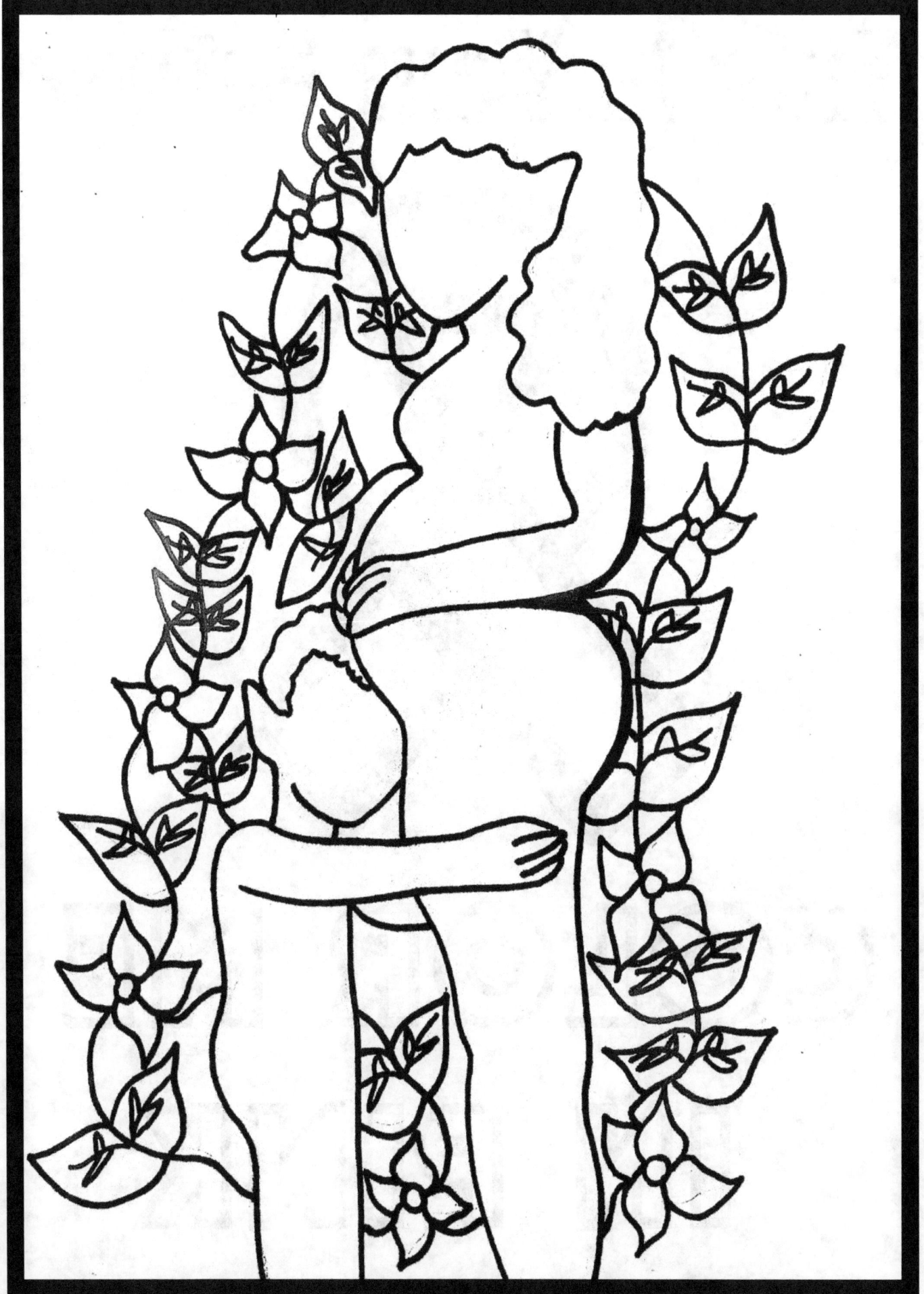

This Is Your Father

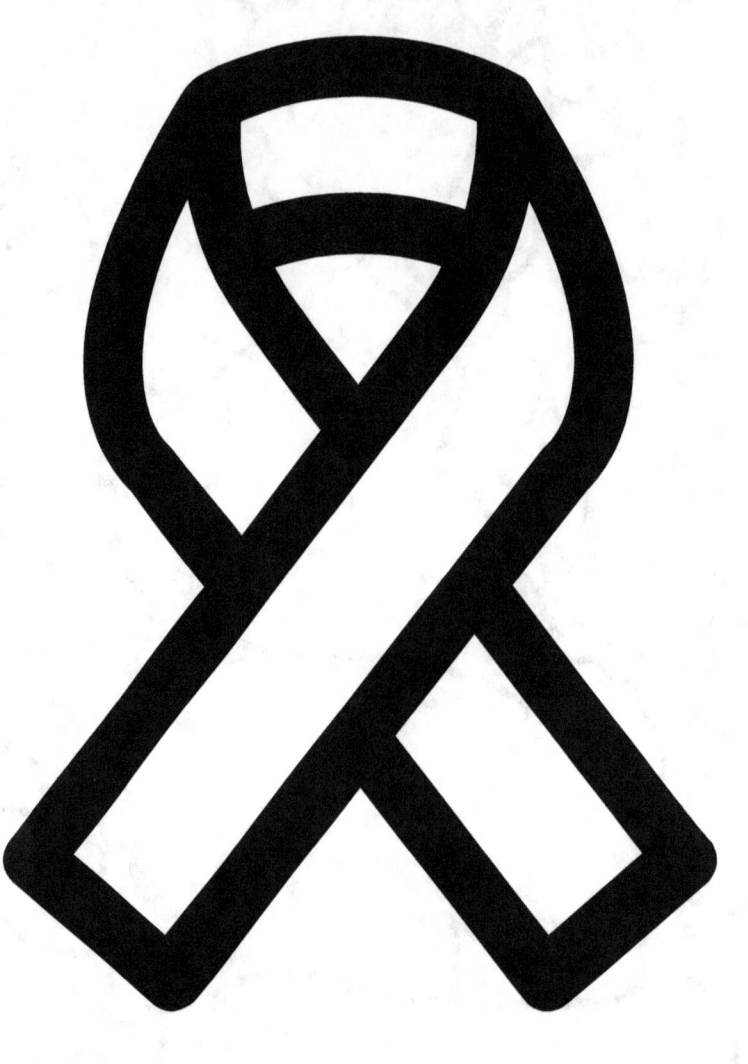

COLOR ME
IN PINK

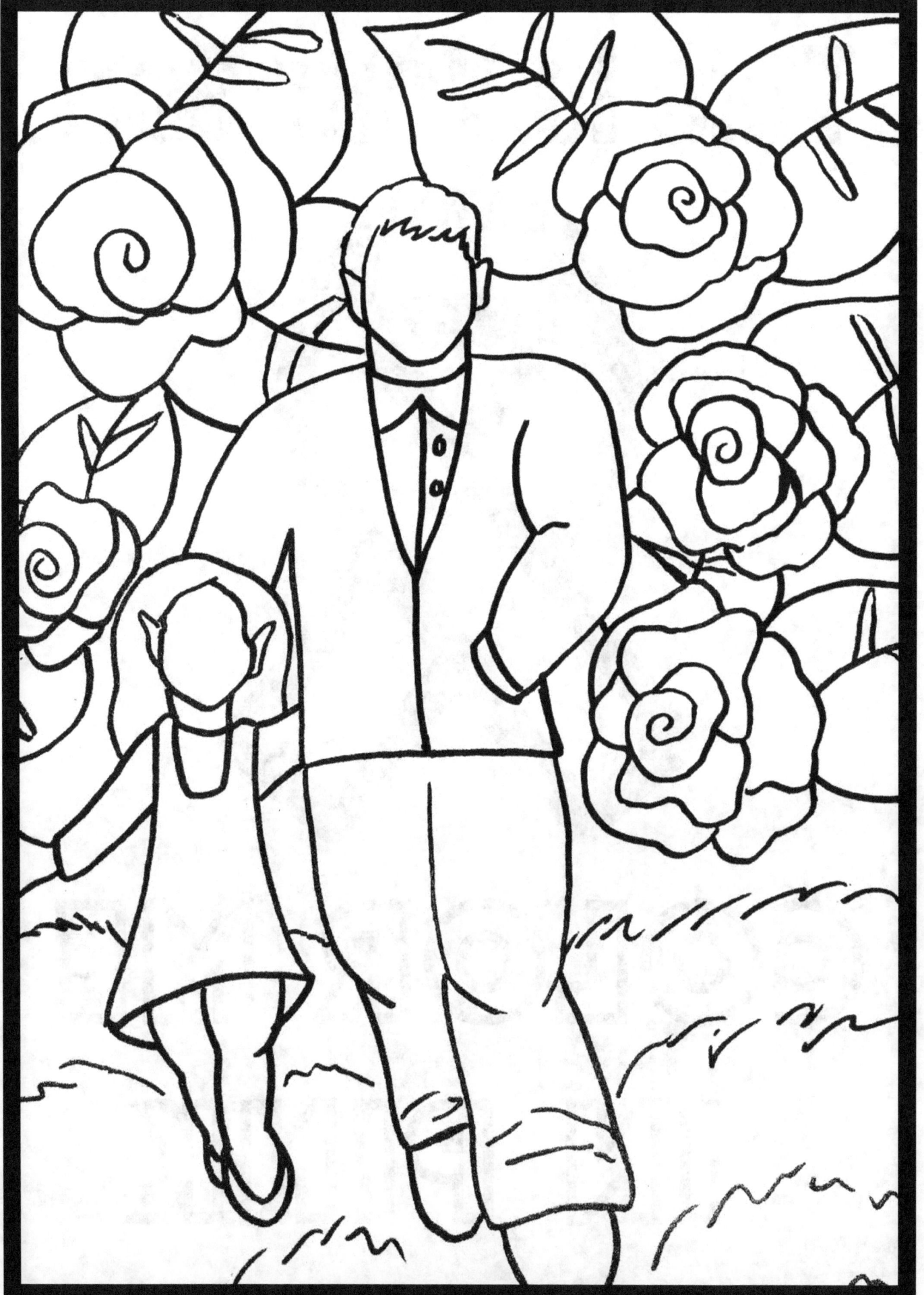

This Is Your Son

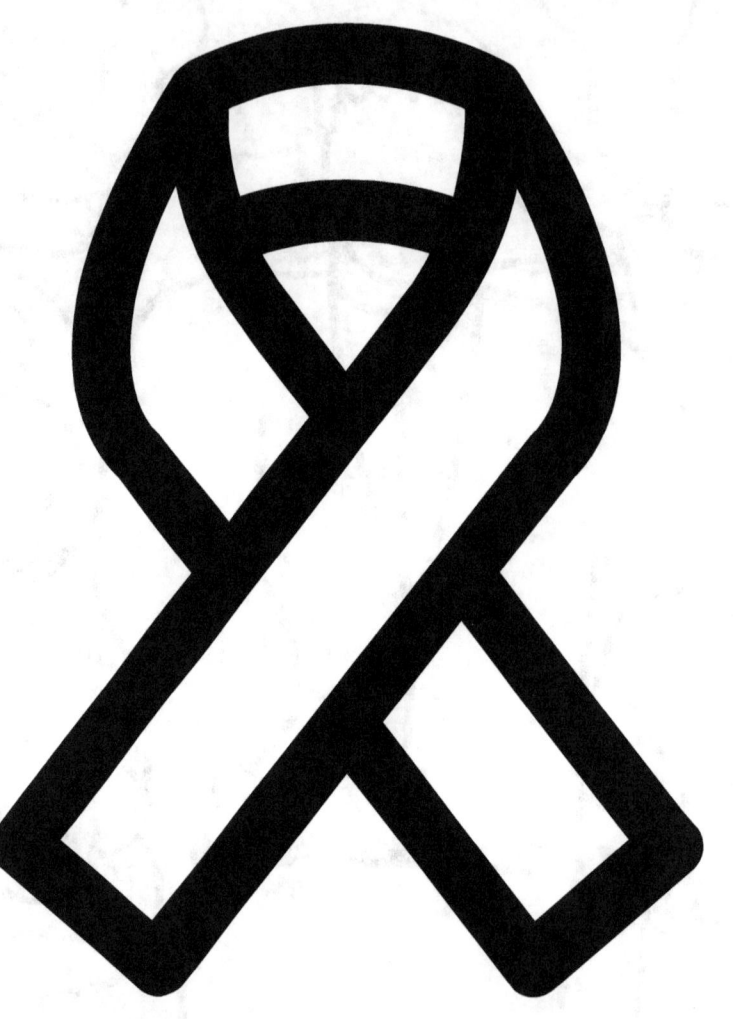

COLOR ME
IN PINK

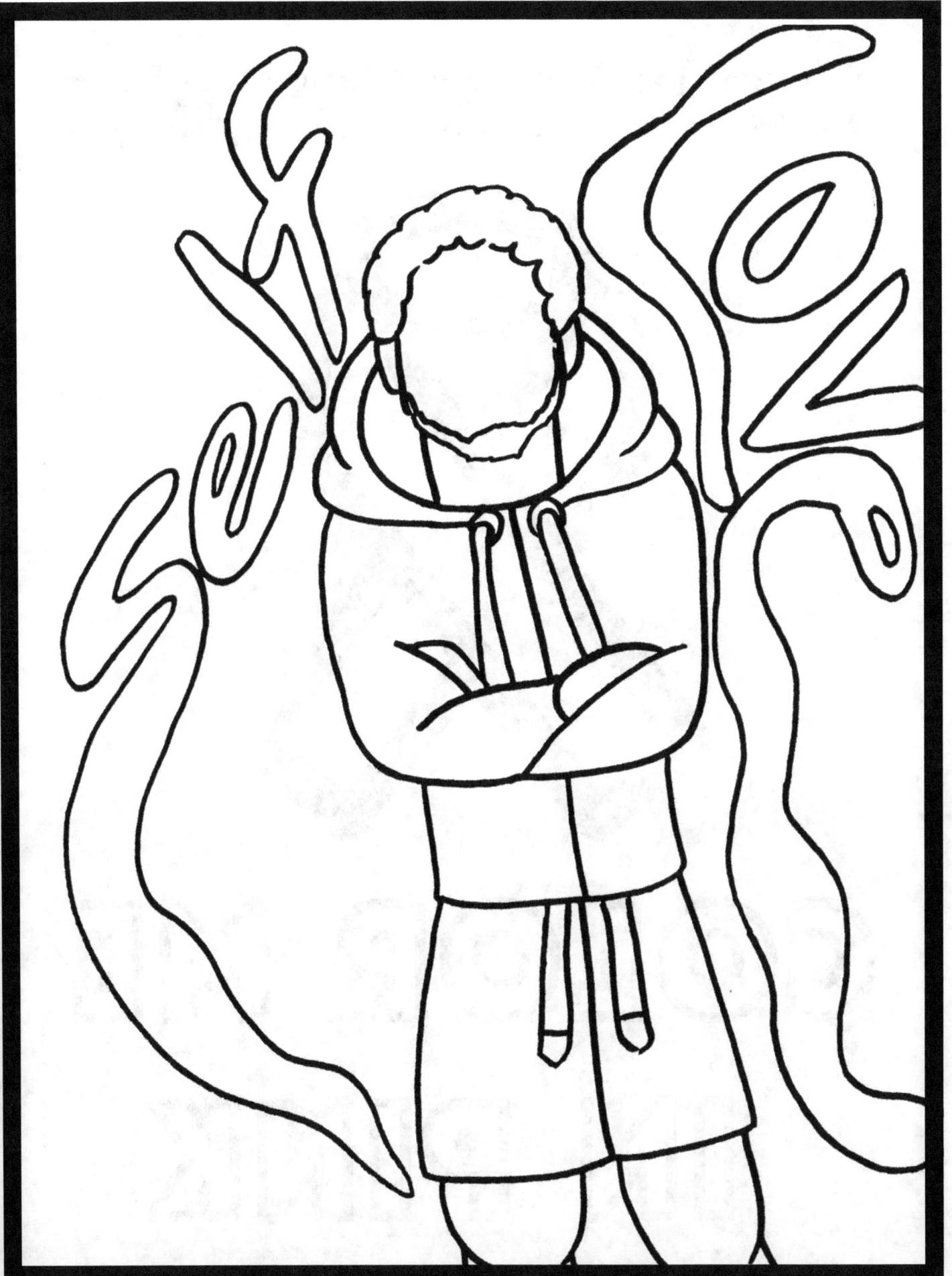

This Is Your Daughter

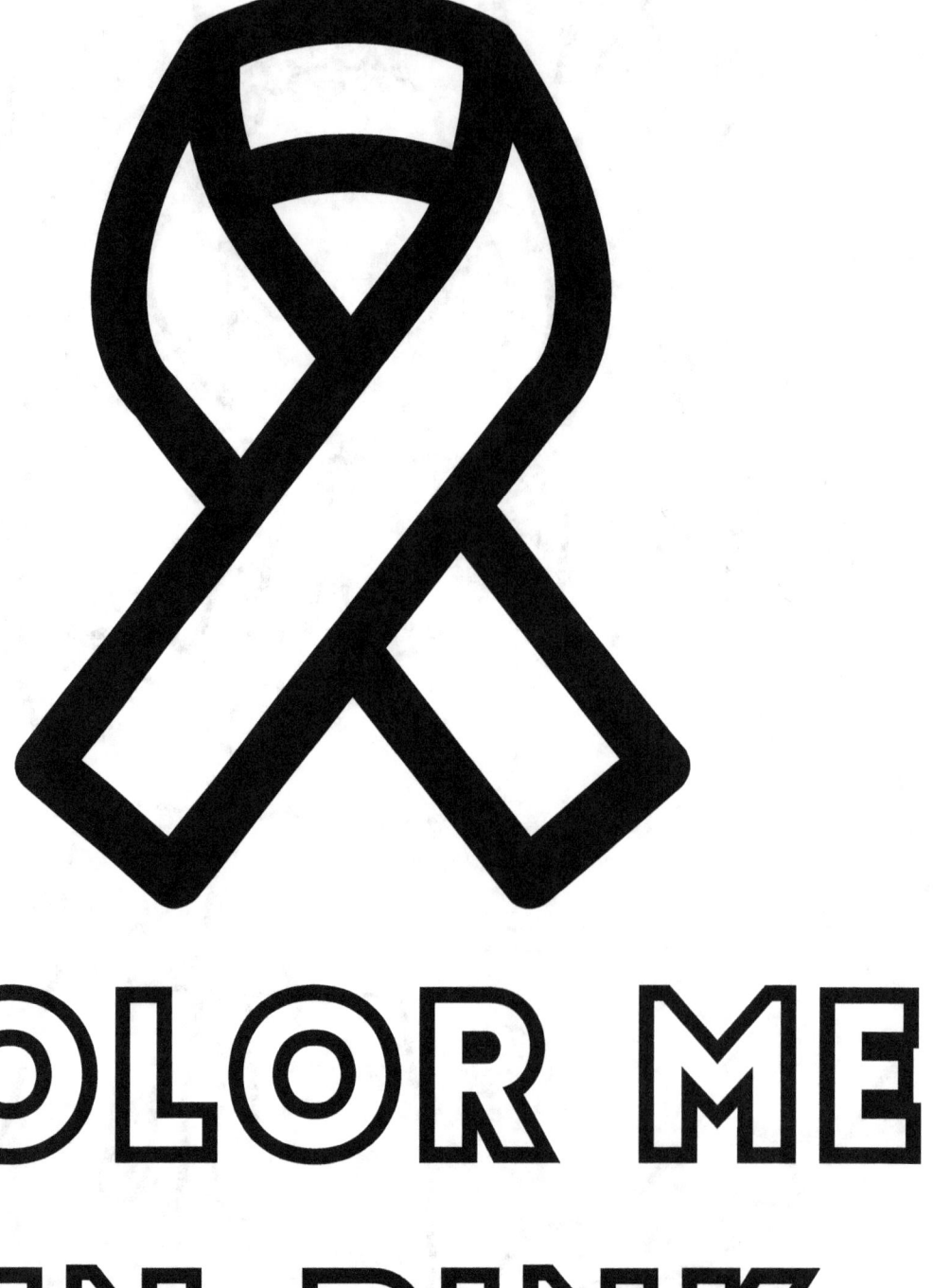

COLOR ME
IN PINK

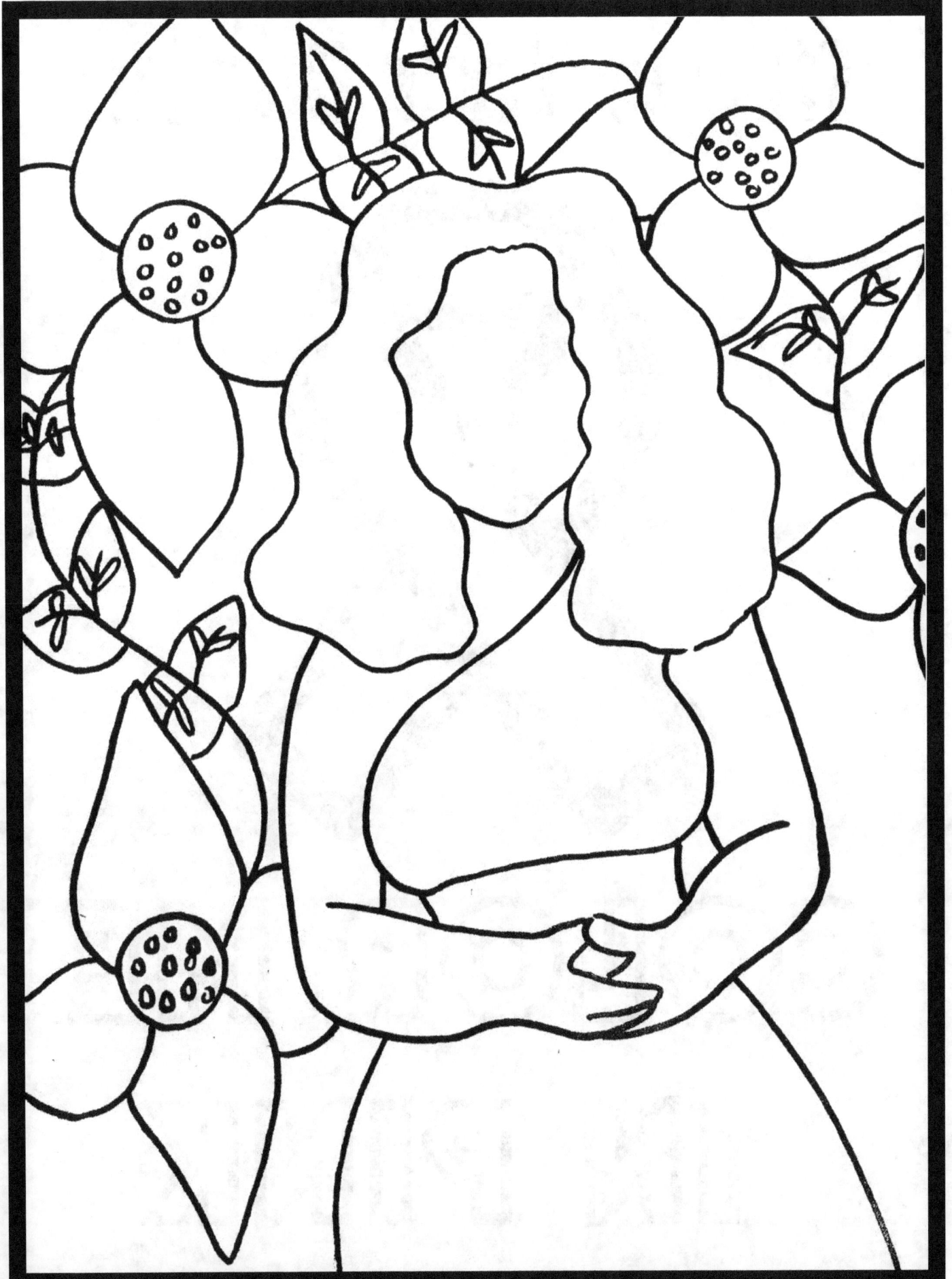

This Is Your Cousin

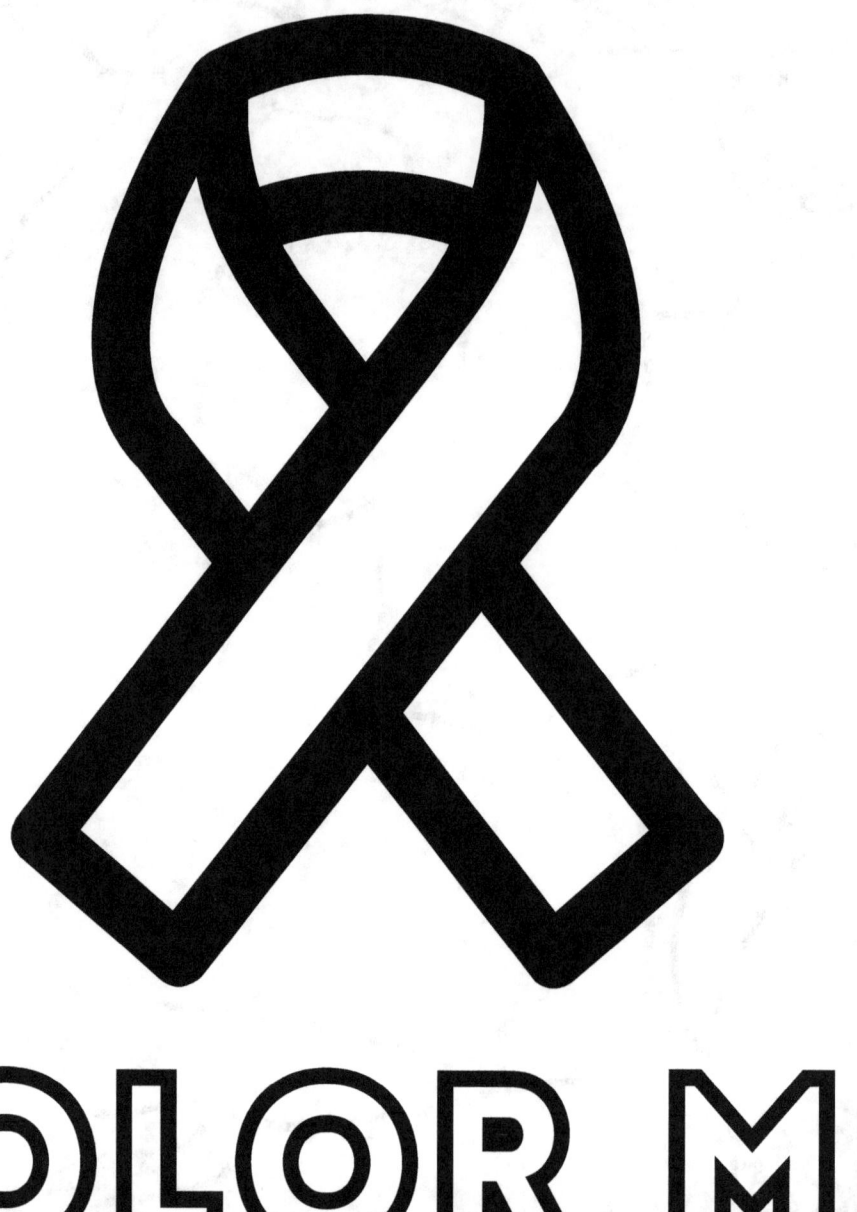

COLOR ME IN PINK

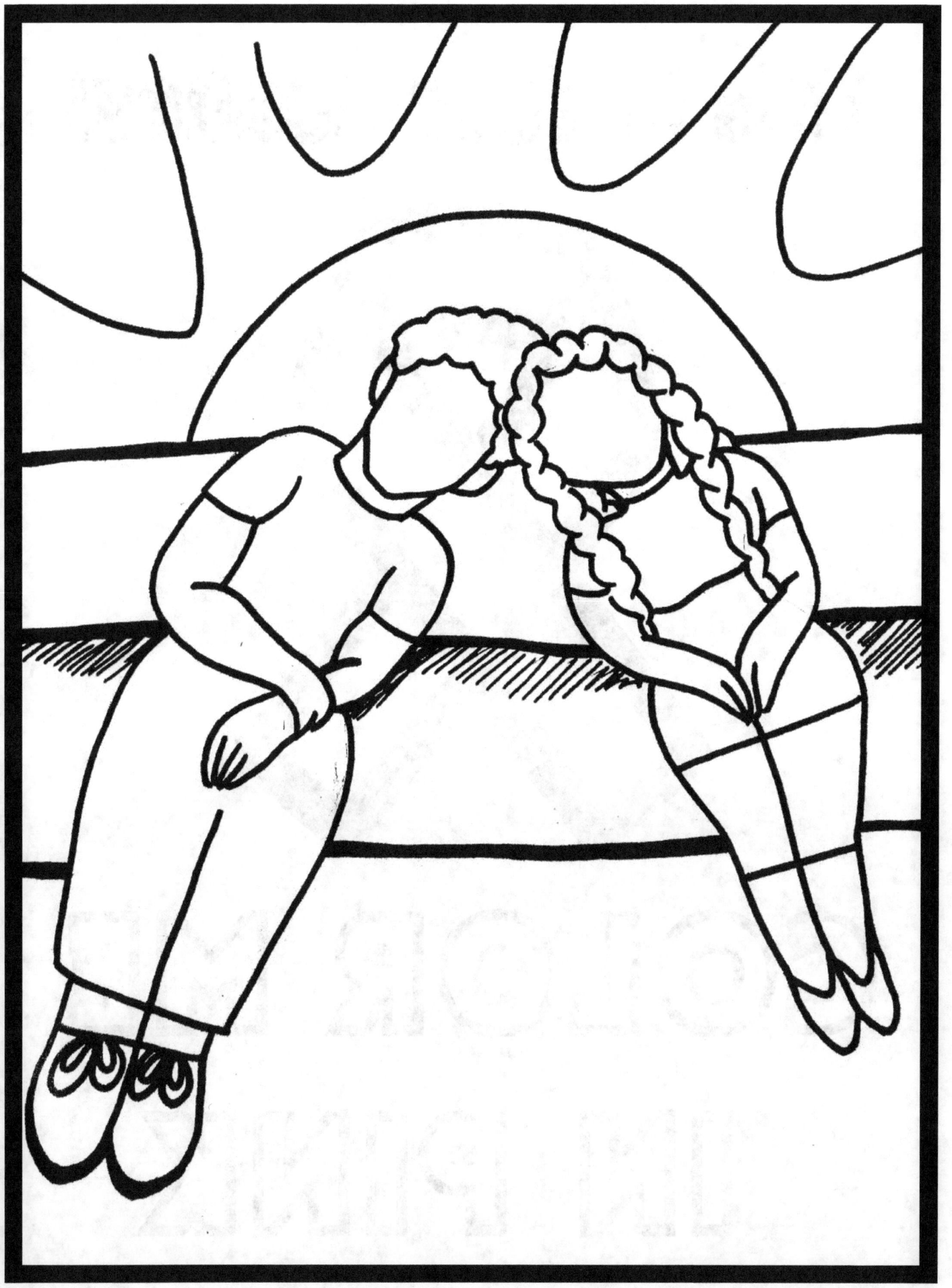

This Is Your Nephew

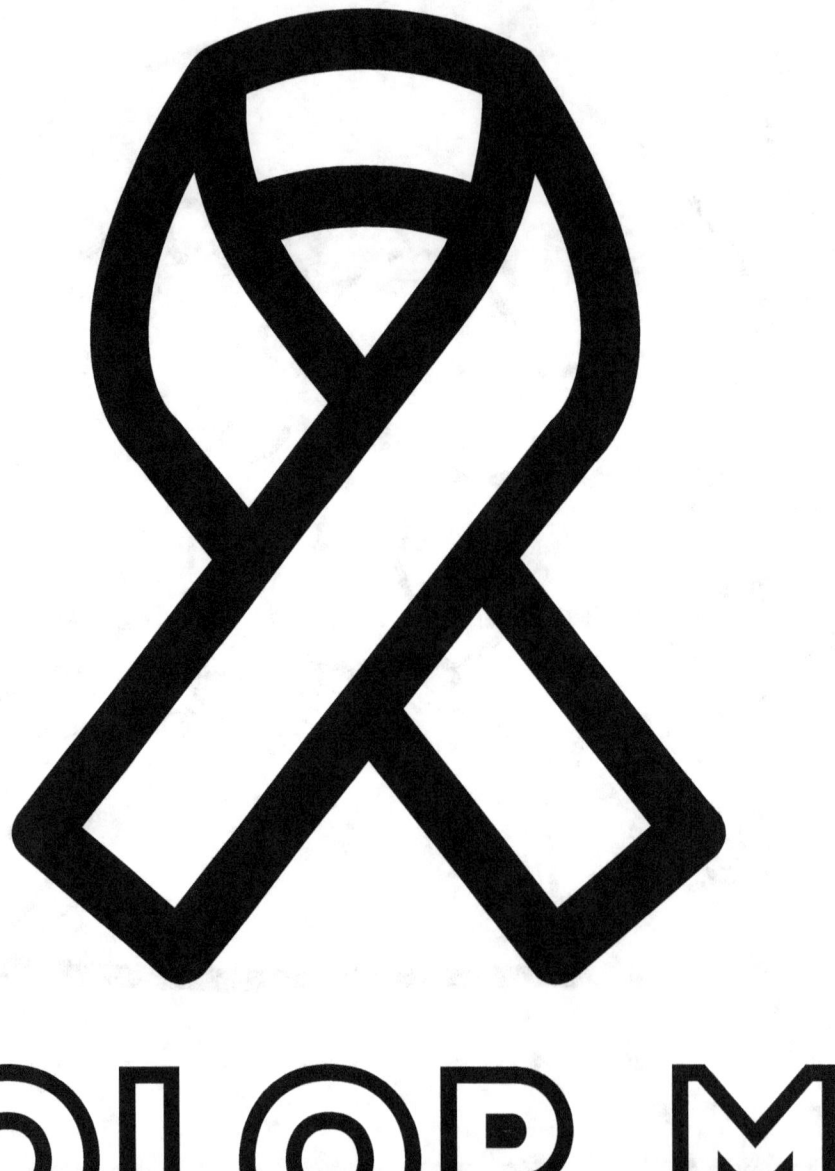

COLOR ME
IN PINK

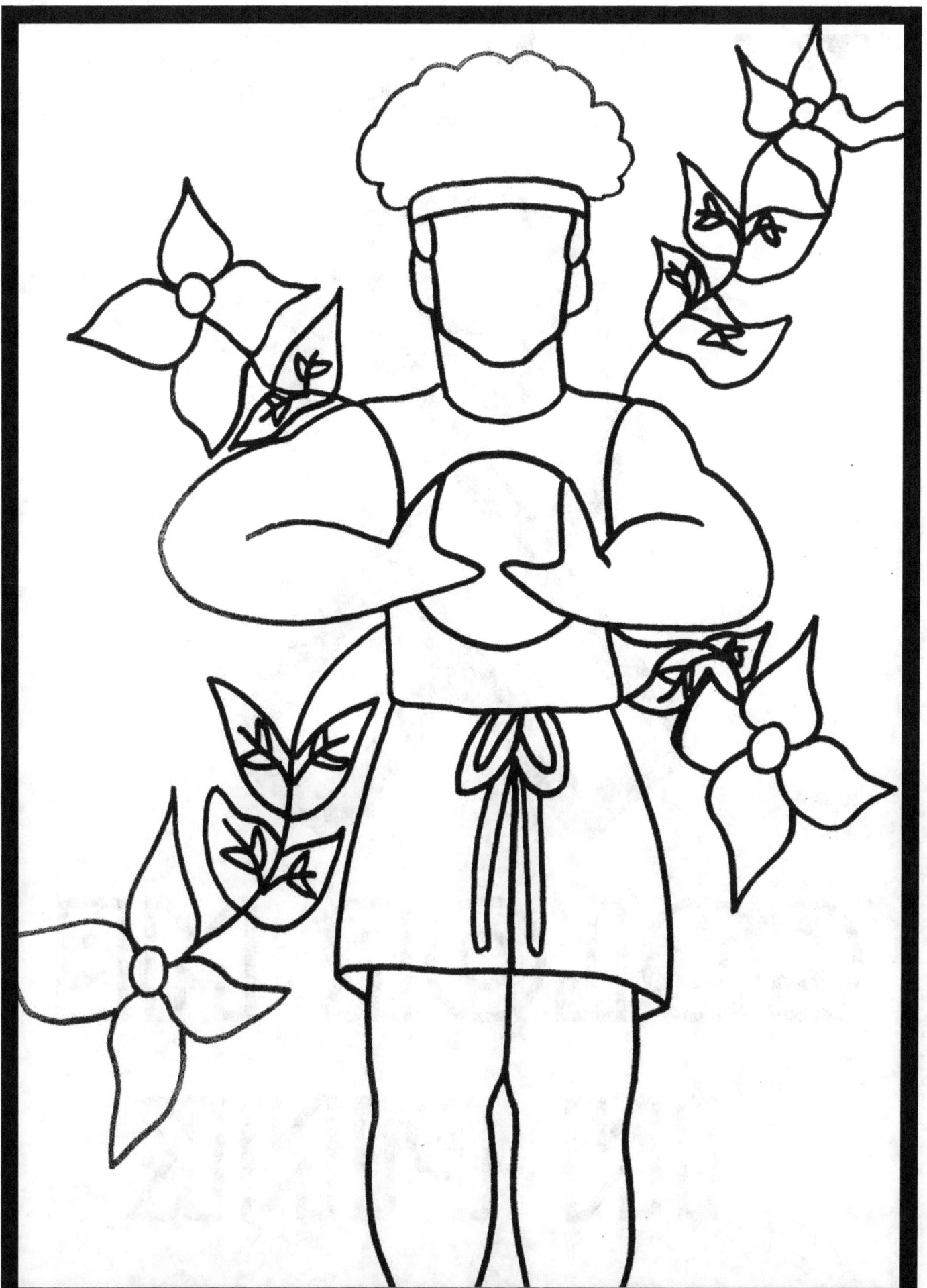

This Is Your Niece

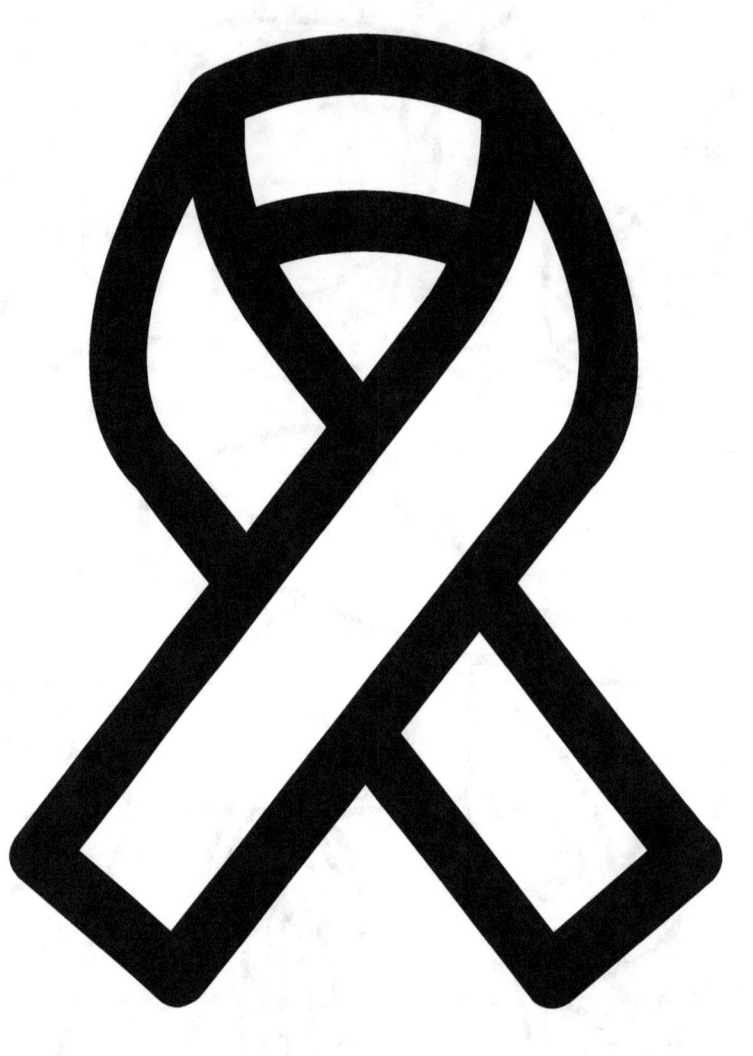

COLOR ME
IN PINK

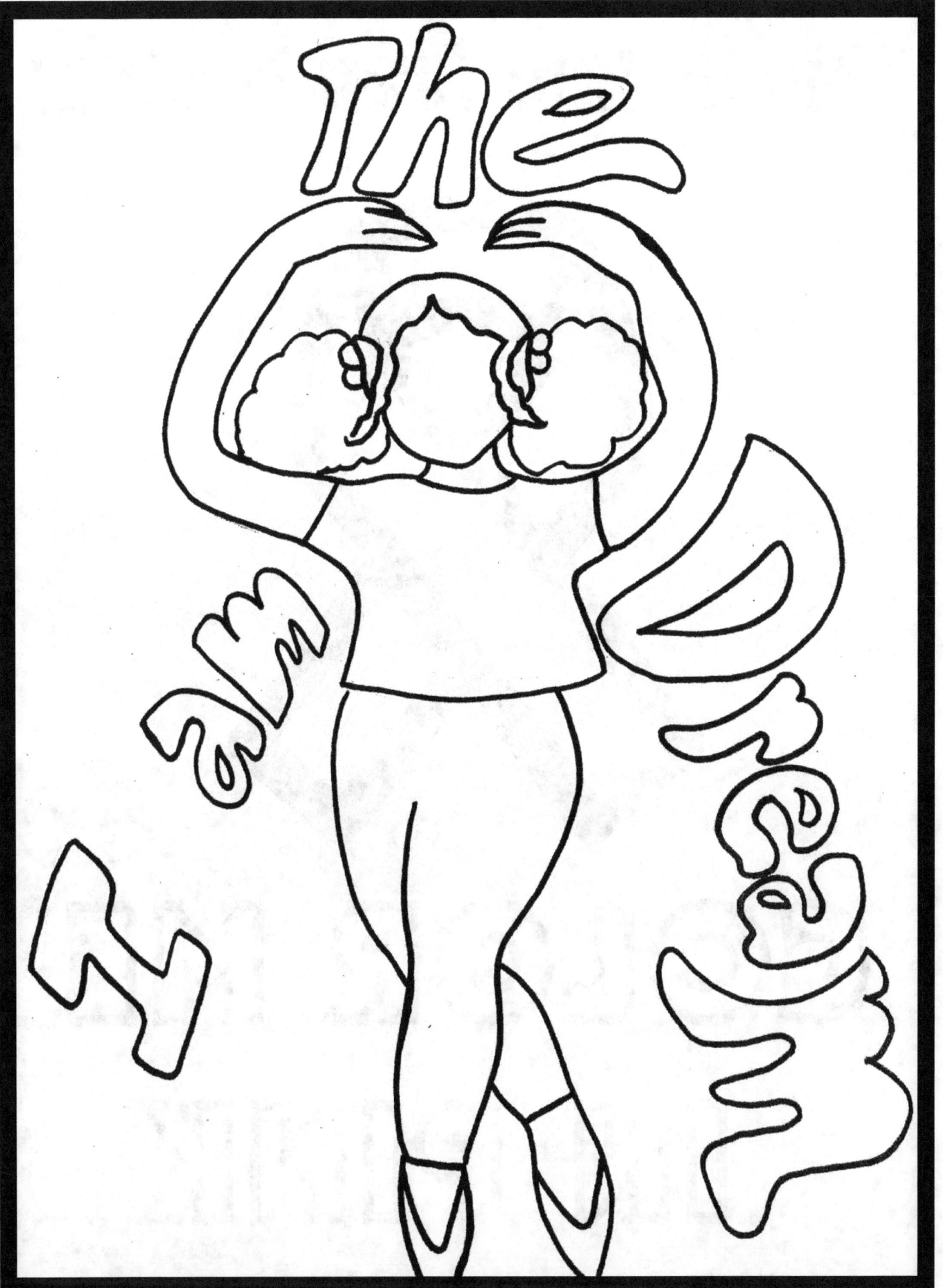

This Is Your Grandmother

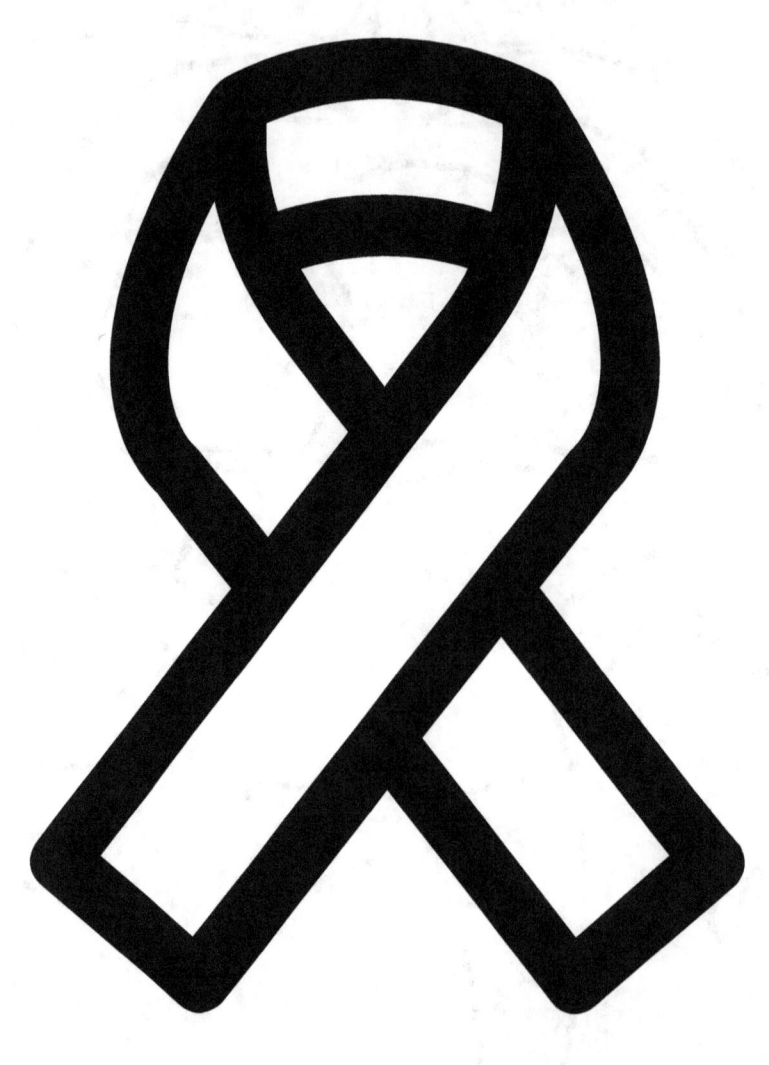

COLOR ME IN PINK

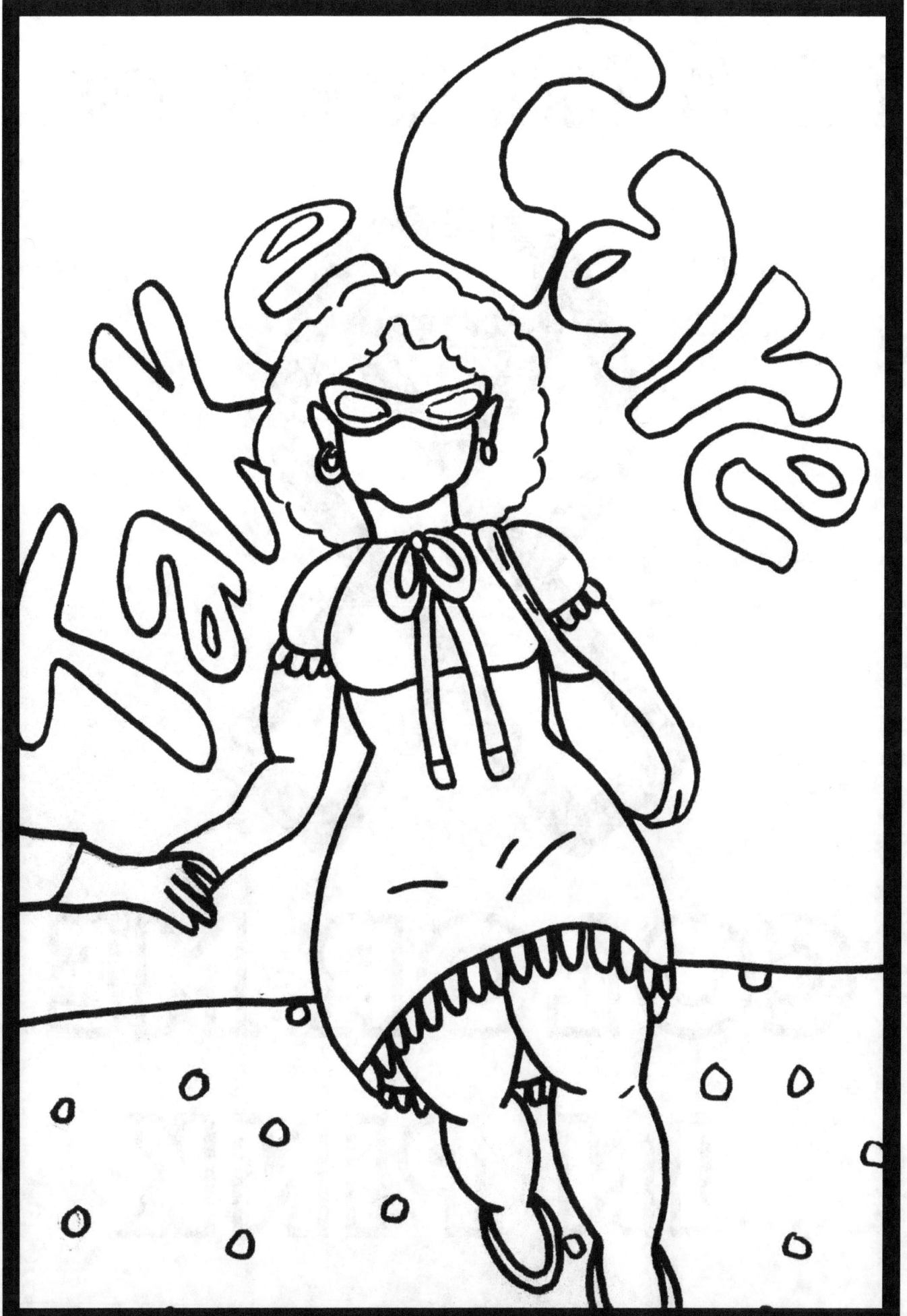

This Is Your Grandfather

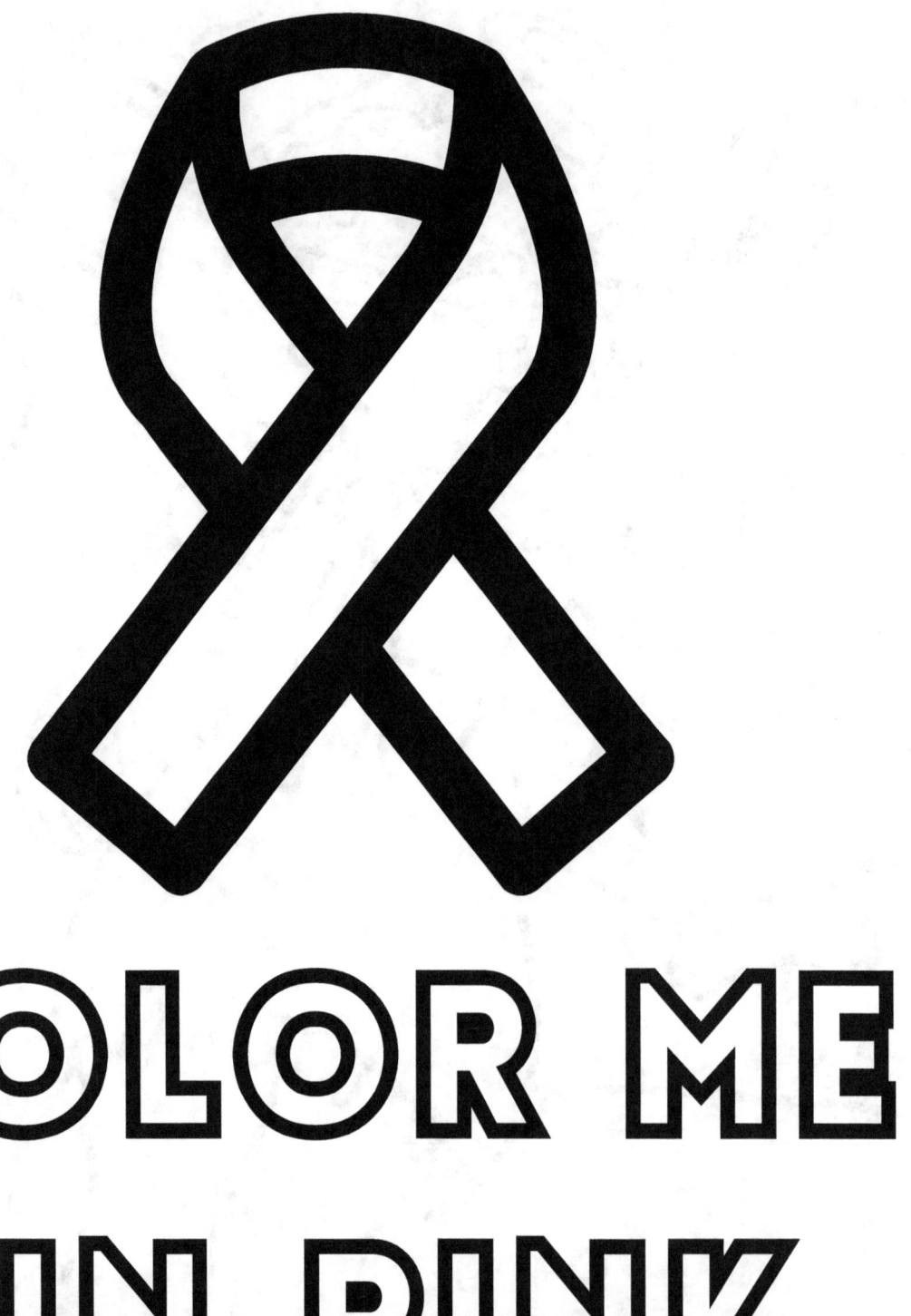

COLOR ME IN PINK

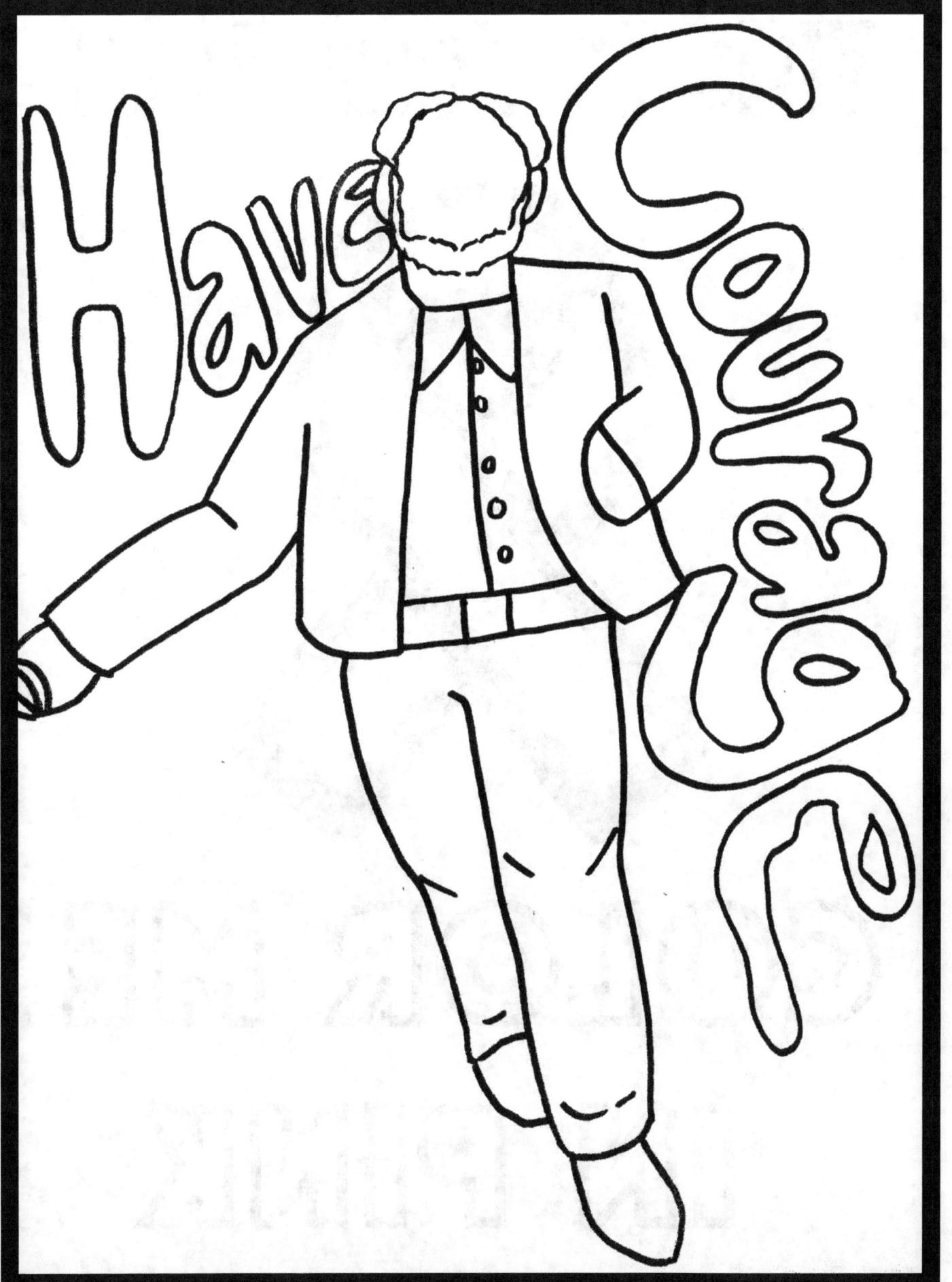

This Is Your Aunt

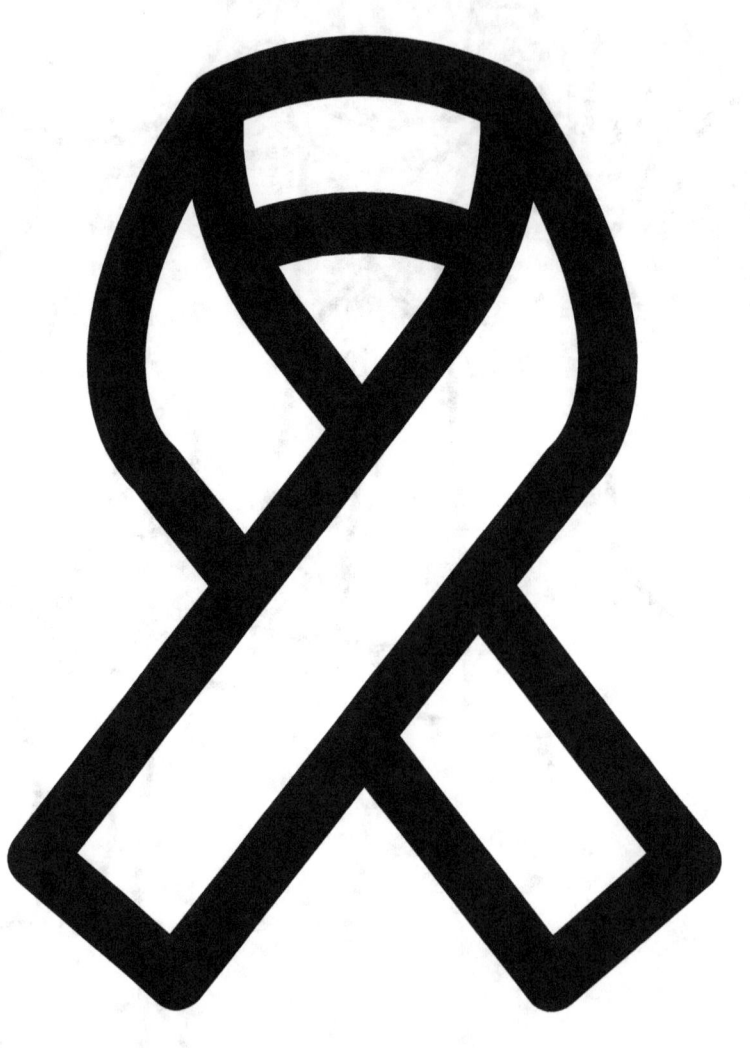

COLOR ME
IN PINK

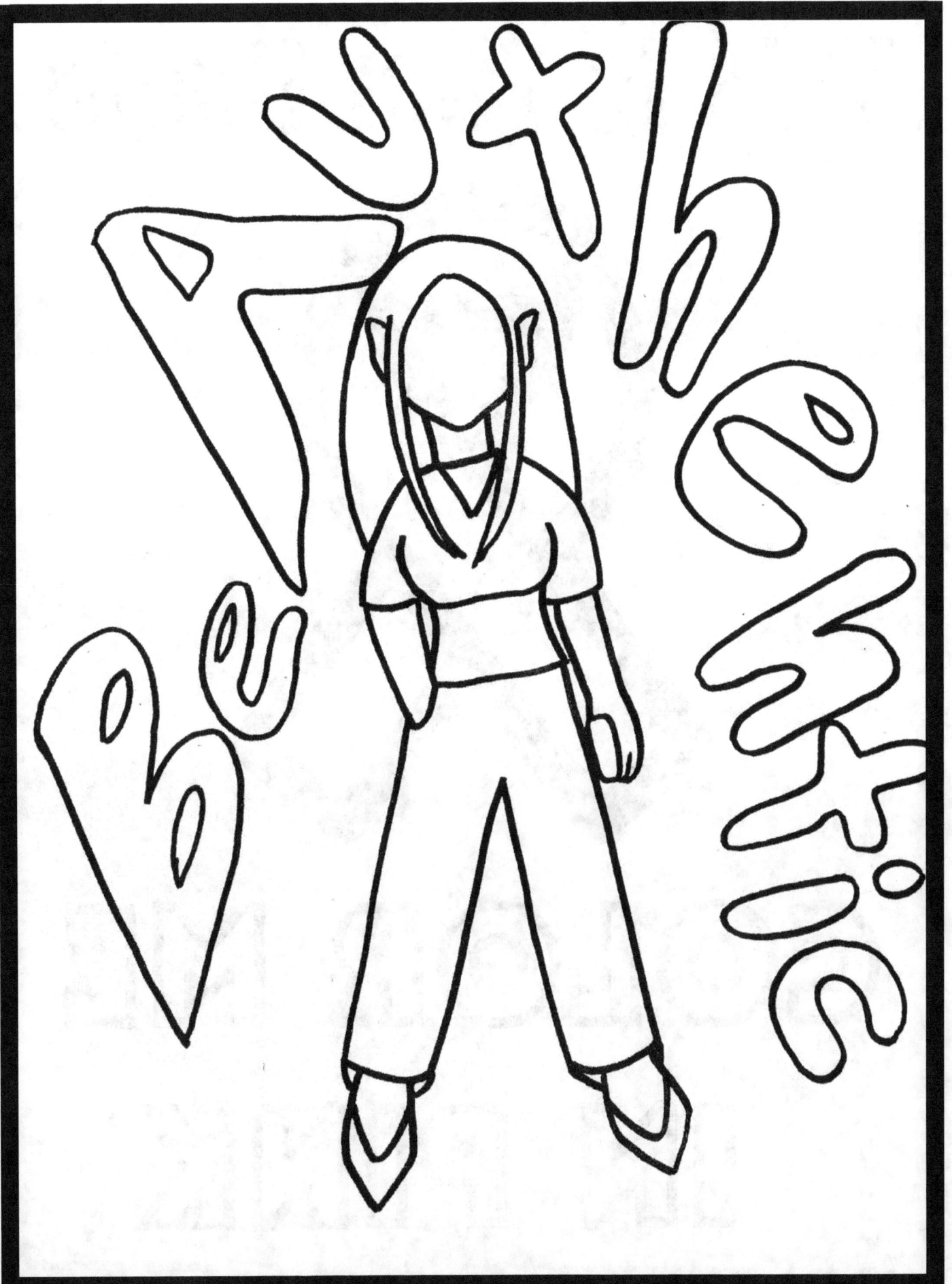

This Is Your Uncle

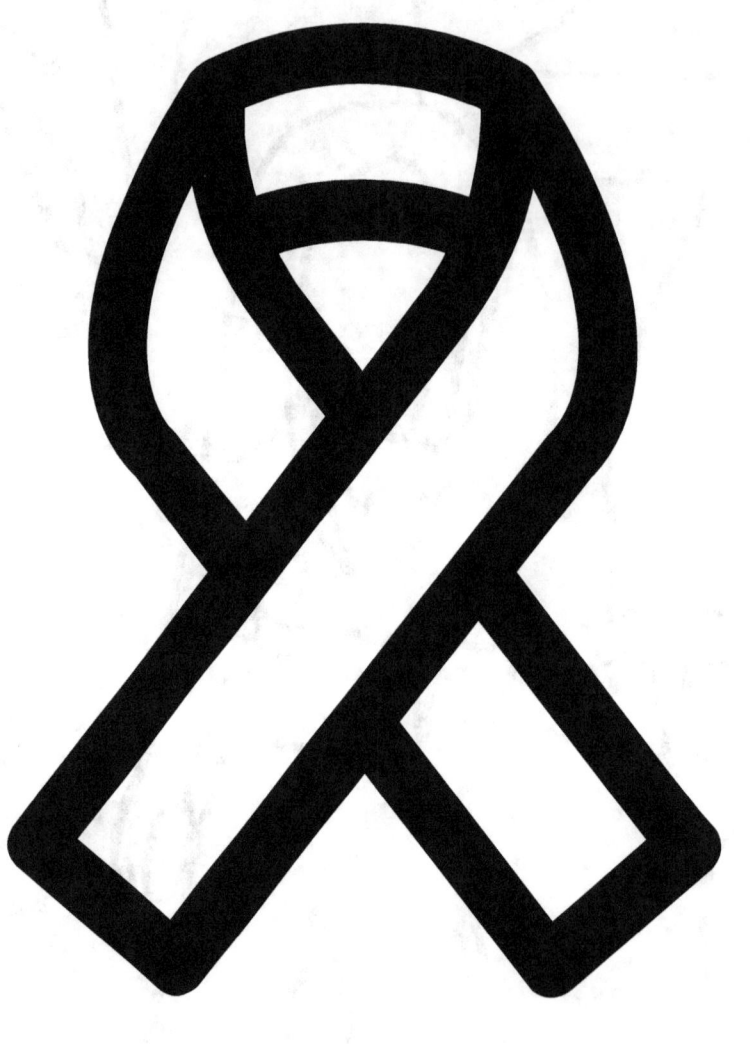

COLOR ME
IN PINK

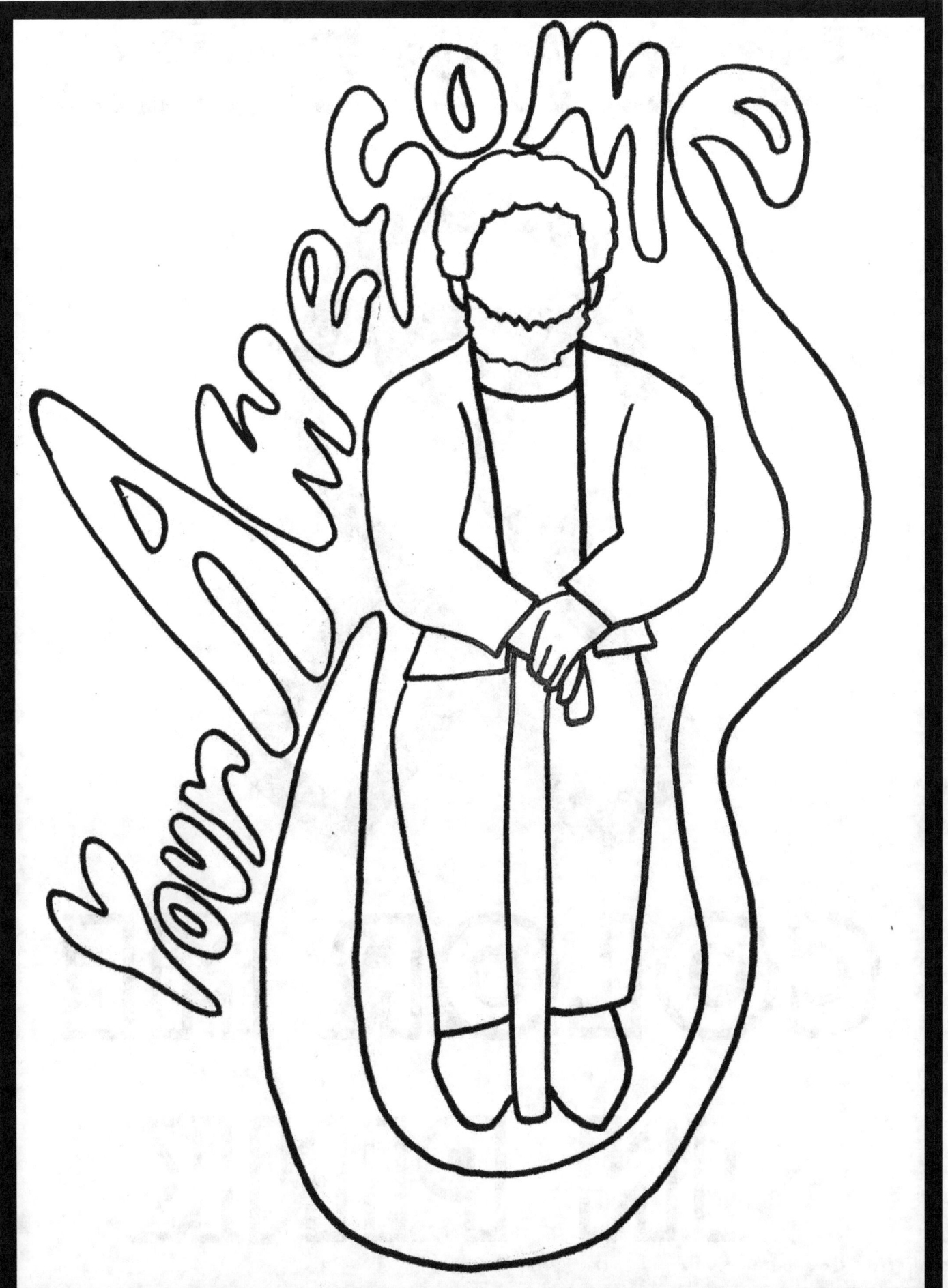

This Is Your Brother

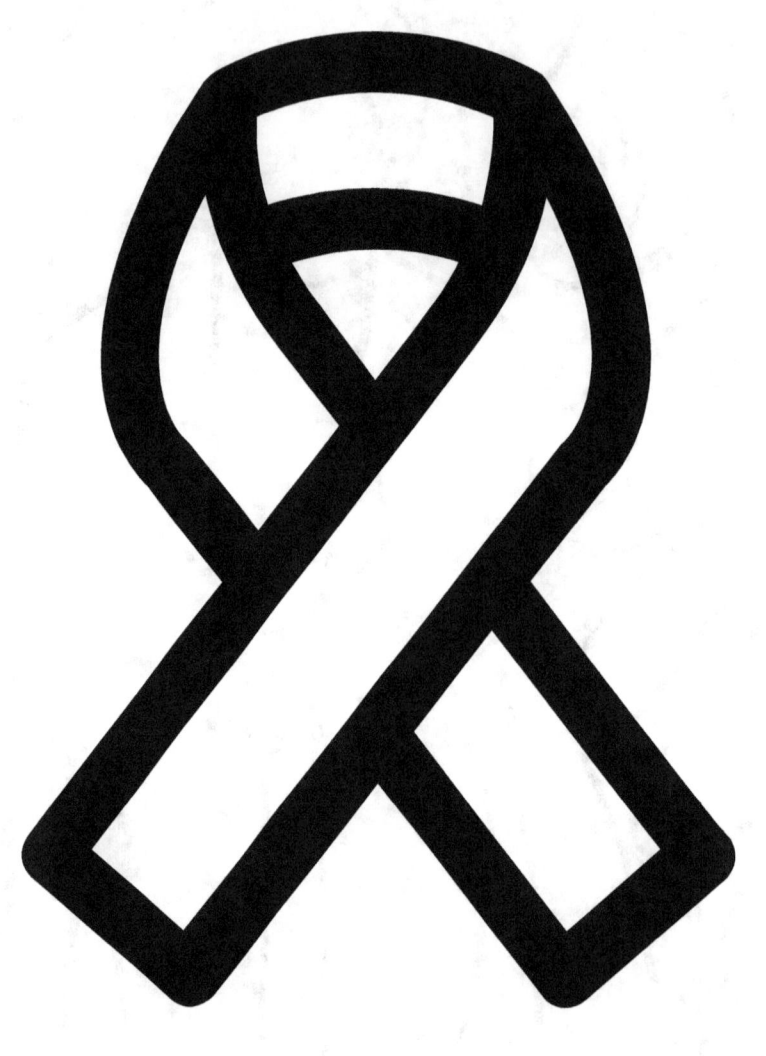

COLOR ME
IN PINK

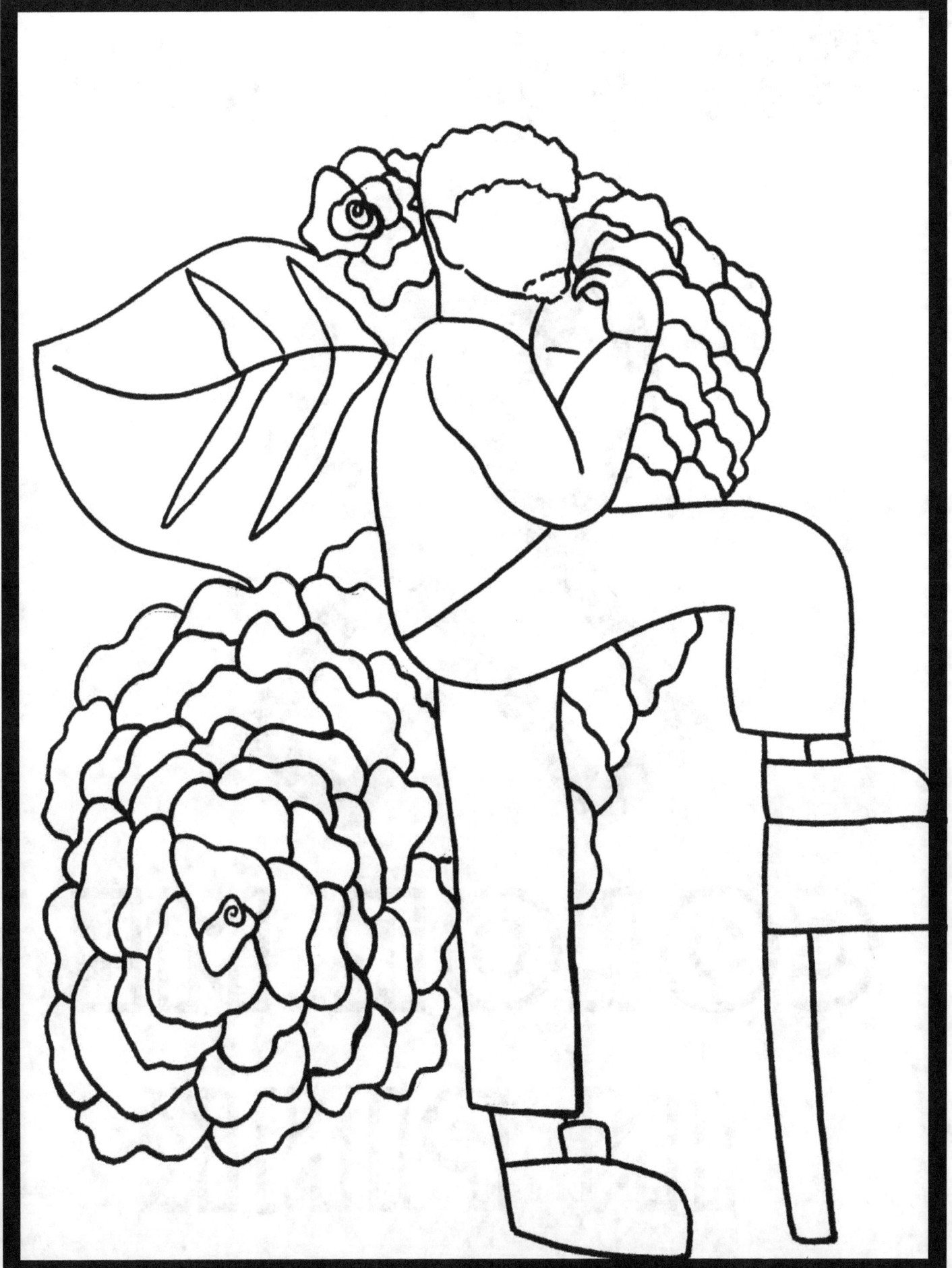

This Is Your Sister

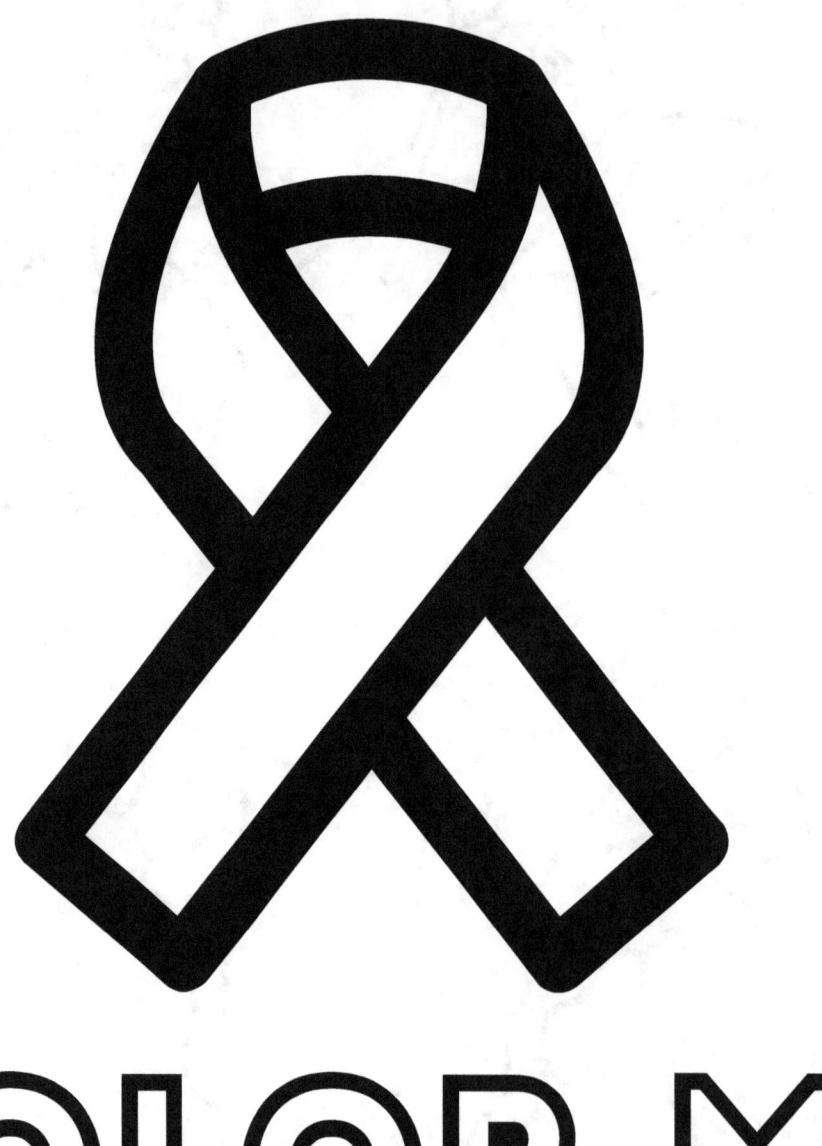

COLOR ME
IN PINK

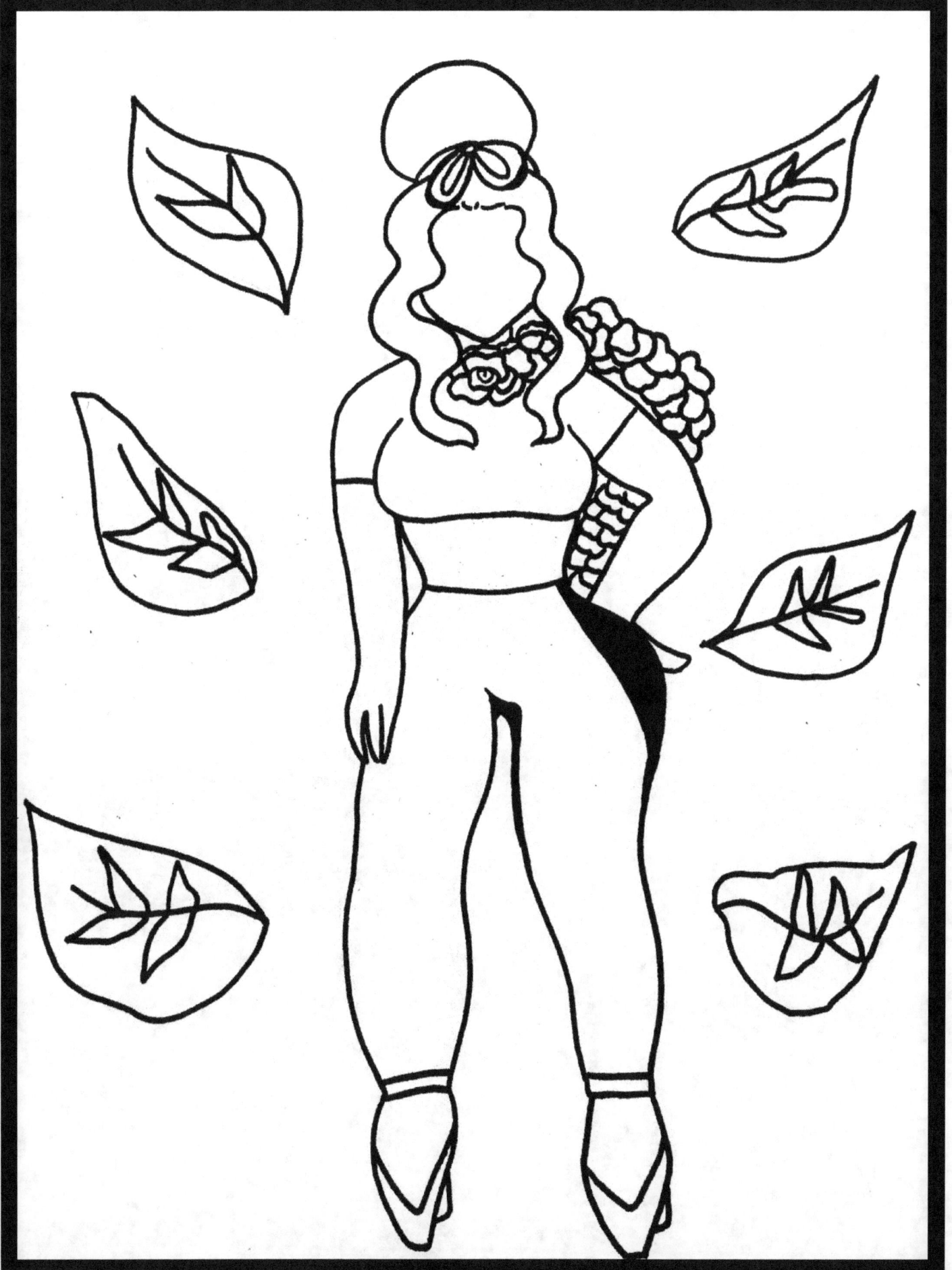

www.ingramcontent.com/pod-product-compliance
Lightning Source LLC
Chambersburg PA
CBHW081709220526
45466CB00009B/2935